IN A
YELLOW
ROOM

IN A
YELLOW
ROOM

Maureen Morehead

The Sulgrave Press
Louisville, Kentucky

For Robert and Clint

ISBN 0-9624086-1-1
Printed in the U.S.A.

Cover design by Louise P. Moremen

ACKNOWLEDGMENTS

Poems in this manuscript have appeared in the following publications:

American Poetry Review	"Shining the Eyes"
The American Voice	"No Room for That"
The Black Warrior Review	"The Purple Lady and God" "The Purple Lady and Mary"
California Quarterly	"It Is What Makes a Woman Not Want to Save Her Own Life"

The Iowa Review	"Emily Dickinson Talks to T. W.
	    Higginson"
	" The Flying-Geese Quilt You'd
	    Brought from Home"

Kansas Quarterly	"This Is Not How Leaving the World is Supposed to Be"
The Louisville Review	"The Laura Poems" "The Purple Lady and Birth" "The Purple Lady and Children" "The Purple Lady and Death" "The Purple Lady and Sexuality" "A Field of Tulips in the Kitchen" "Lessons" "What I Thought Was a Birdhouse Is Really a Lamp" "If You'd Married Edgar Degas"
Poet and Critic	"At First, Mary Cassatt"

The author wishes to thank the Kentucky Arts Council and the Kentucky Foundation for Women for grants that helped her complete this collection.

These poems are about the modern woman's journey toward meaning through a life filled with husbands, children, friends, work, conflicts, fears, decisions, fantasies, and dreams. They are imagaic, tough, and moving poems, blending lyric and narrative, light and dark, the actual and fictional. They are poems that look at the world squarely, see the violence and injustice, but affirm, too, a world where the balance of powers is possible, where the creative process itself lends insight, and where life, and the preservation of it, are sacred.

CONTENTS

THE LAURA POEMS

GOING BACK
for Laura, a friend

1

I have never lived where the leaves fall,
where my face falls into the brown garden.
I am a sexless angel, or the sex of an angel.
I do everything in brown —
my hair, the walls, the tree
I bend around my wrist for a bracelet.

The seasons change again and again.
It is autumn.
Birds with white feathers have flown south.
I, too, would fly south were it not
for the brown of these walls and time,
for the white face of a child at my window.
He is yet to be conceived.

2

We are dancing in the black eye of a needle;
we sit talking. Young. Girls.
It is cold out. I see the old stone silo
from your window, falling leaves.
I rest my face in your hands.

Laura, you are all my sisters,
the white-haired gymnast clicking
her body through air,
the artist in the mirror,
and your voice is a violin
exploring the negative of angel,
the soul of the beech leaves falling.

THE WHITE BIRD

It was autumn and part of winter.
The gingko tree dropped its leaves
in one night. I knew a bird
with white wings who sang
us into his body.

There was a wall. Your mother sat
on the bed, telling her visions. We flew
into the wall — you , I, the white bird,
a boy —
until we had pushed our baptisms
back into the dark.

Gingko leaves are the color of sun and peaches.
Heavy. They burn our eyes on looking.
Blackbirds roost in gray branches.

The ritual of retracting your baptism
is like stripping the blackbirds
of their oils. So they cannot fly; so they
die in the cold. You don't realize guilt
sticks on your clothes, like smoke, heavier
than oil, until it's over.

We burn leaves. Someone — is it you?
is it I? — offers a porcelain angel
to the white flames. I vision
an angel burns with such height
no one hears her screaming.

I wipe the black from her forehead, kiss
the white, clean spot.
Laura offers a lullaby, her voice is dark.
A blackbird with the throat of an oboe
sings the elegy.

LEARNING THE VOICES OF BIRDS

1

They come into my room, young men
talking of Nietzsche, of the morals
lost in our generation.
Some play war games: "I'm Robert E. Lee
at 4 today." I nod. They think I know.
I know their bird-colored faces,
the way they casually drop their arms,
walk out.

2

There was an ice storm
the day of the wedding. Lucky we
put it off until March.
Redbirds came to the grass
to feed that month.
"I'd do it again in a second,"
I tell you after
and mean it.

The quail lay dead in your hand,
brown, beige specked, no blood,
its head limp: "first one
of the season."
Once we made love under a spruce.
I shook my arms. Soft green needles
fell to the ground.

3

All winter they flew into the plate glass.
Smashed heartbeats and breastbones.
Birds in our heads. So Laura says
she's into jazz, writing her own songs
now at 30. I step
into her glass blue eyes. Freeze.
I do not write a word for years.

4

It's important you're careful what you say
to them, the young men:
"come meet my friend Laura
with the green, green eyes."

I can think of no one perfect time
for making love.
I can think of no one perfect time
for learning the strange voices of birds
in the forest.

POEM WRITTEN IN SPRING

Laura surrounds herself with beautiful
women. Laura's men are wizards and geniuses.
Laura loves young boys with thin necks
and rat-colored eyes, a black man
in a tall black gown.
Laura loves the birds.

It's been years since we were girls
in Lexington. I watched her
brush her white hair at the mirror,
her eyes slip from wedgwood to grass,
years since college,
since the deaths we knew
each winter would bring.

We know better now.
In Boston, in Mississippi, wherever you are,
Laura, there is no particular time for dying.

It is spring
and the beautiful blonde boy
is slipping out of his bones,
climbing like a fragile airplane to avoid
the rain, steady rain of the season.
How sad watching a boy become the house
where glows the wisdom of God,
how sad we're left to remember, to wait,
to attempt closing fissures in our lives with time.

ALONE: A FRAGMENT

And there is a time when the leaves
are down, mulched underfoot.
I try not to see winter as an end,
but it is November, and has already snowed.
My husband travels places
I have never known, and I ask, where am I?
I wear no jewelry, my face is plain
in the silence of a house.

If winter were a woman,
her veins could lace through me,
a veil and a face and my brown hair
tangle in white. Is it true
I married him?
It is difficult to remember those things
which almost happen. It is difficult
to remember those persons
who were almost here.

In the middle of the night
when he lays his hand on my hand,
I am sure for a while that nothing really changes,
but there are the months, the months
we live through as if they are unnecessary rooms.
I slip into the neck of a tree.
There it is dark. There brown and white
are the same color.
My husband leaves the house
before the snow is finished falling.

WITH A MAN

I thought I could read the trees
in fall, particularly the beech trees. Roots
above ground are in my nature, and
leaves pressed to the pavement by rain.

For years you held me up in the sky
with the palms of your eyes.
With respect to stars you said
I shine.

I am a woman.
I am old enough to have children. Tell Laura
I'll cut up the wedding album,
sell the brown of my eyes back to the earth.
I must cross the Barren River
and the Green River. I must sell my gloss
for profit.

There's this fondness for wild things,
a part of the bargain, a photograph of you
holding a leaf-colored rabbit
in the cup of your hands.
We were married a month,
I kiss you as always.

Even you know this:
home is across two rivers and I'll need
a ferryman. Perhaps it is not time.
Perhaps it is better to put wild things off.

In the water of the river I watch my hair
gray to bark, rain silver when I bend
my eyes. I'll bear you a child.
I'll wait for winter.
I'll bear you a child; I'll wait for winter.

QUILTS

SHINING THE EYES

for Rebecca Bryant Boone

The hills of Kentucky arch their backs like whales.
Daniel Boone mistook you, a child, for a deer
one night on a fire-hunt. Your eyes shoved him
out of the dark. He married you, then took you west
with everything you owned in an old sea-chest: candles,
bowls, a letter in your mother's handwriting, clothes
in boxes, and seed.   Consider gardens, Daniel said,
then slipped you through a gap in a mountain.
Everywhere were cedar and shade. When he talked to you,
even then, there was departure in his throat.
The scent of marriage had worn off
by the time you were eighteen.

Actually you met him at your sister's wedding.
He was five feet six and did not wear a coonskin cap.
I married Daniel Boone too. The day after,
riding down the Western Kentucky Parkway
in his '68 Volkswagen, he turned to me
and remembered his fishing rod. The bridal quilt
should have been pine-trees, spruce and white,
trees as tall as hills wherever you looked.
Instead it was a plain of sand dollars, white on blue
or blue on white. Blue water of the Atlantic,
snow-covered fields of Illinois.
I've admitted nothing.

When I was seventeen, I promised to wear his name
like skin. At thirty-five, I am part quail,
dove, grouse, rabbit, dirt, salt,
pheasant, and deer. You have to know me for a long time
to see animals in my eyes: the silence they make,
the racket, uncalculated snapping,
white-tipped tails, then air.

CRAZY QUILT

"Jan. 1, 1902: Can it be that I have reached the age of 40?"
                                       Sallie Crain Garr, Kentucky Quilts

A scrawny little boy,
a lobster,
a tractor on the highway,
Amish red, a parachute, war,
a cow you can name
the name of your enemy,
or better yet, your fear,
the first black iron skillet,
1928, the metaphor comparing sex
and jazz, a flu-shot,
syndrome, mathematician,
flock of turkeys,
memorandum, a tree
in winter not blooming,
bulbous, pear-shaped,
or young.

Here is the list.
I am giving back what
has been given to me. Equipment,
armor, a field of cows named
spider, blank, germ,
insignificance, lust, and slip.
Death is an allergy,
a brown dress, an antidote,
a milky bone. Next is the garden.
Stringbean, earth, a marigold.

AFTERIMAGE

1

The wheel is central to the quilt.
Its spokes are the grass
a wagon can move through like water,
and mud, frustration of losing time and lost
possessions. I see a woman in brown furrows
outside the vast wheel, blocks of wool:
Oregon, Arkansas, Kansas, Michigan,
and Maine. The woman is tending
a thousand crops. There are blackbirds
in the corn, sometimes giant sycamores
scaring them off. In Kentucky, the tobacco
has been harvested and is drying upside-down
in barns.

2

The woman is looking directly at the wheel.
She neither shields her eyes
nor looks away. The sun this day is a tomato,
a zinnia, a daylily, a redware platter
large as a whale's skull. Unlike the wheel,
the sun has legs, and the potential
to bring us in like a lighthouse.
The wheel determines. The sun encourages.
It is the difference between the day
a woman knows she cannot leave,
and the day she knows
she can.

THE FLYING-GEESE QUILT YOU'D BROUGHT FROM HOME

for Priscilla Beaulieu Presley

One day in 1965 when I was struggling with angles,
with making things fit, determining x and eliminating y,
Elvis Presley locked the two of you in his bedroom
and didn't let you out for a week.
He liked it cold. He liked the TV on.
He liked you nude, and pure, fifteen years old,
dumb as a bologna sandwich.

You remember lying in bed,
a quilt with a thousand triangles up to your breasts,
your breasts exposed because he liked to look at you,
happy that he looked at you, counting the triangles,
losing track, a shadow at the bedroom door,
two bowls of tomato soup.

I was in love then, too, in Kentucky, and kissed a boy
from California with a beautiful name,
and when he had gone I thought about him for months.
I kissed him in September. A cold breeze had come up.
It was under a streetlamp. His mouth felt warm on mine.
If I imagined him in my bed, it was I who submitted.
Those days every one of us knew the equation:
his name fit perfectly after mine.

A HOUSE ON THE RIVER WITH NO FRONT YARD

Even as children, we knew the house
was not intended for us.
When we were there,
suntanned to the waist, and busy,
the couple, who had no children of their own,
worried about the verandah,
how if we fell,
there would be no saving us,
how water muffles light and noise. The house
rocked on a bed of blue water. It was white
and the water was blue. And, thinking back,
no one seemed very happy there. Sometimes
when we were older, visiting, my aunt would talk
about giant redwoods she had seen in California
when she was a girl, how they were as old
as anything had ever been, how the Pacific
was mad, but when Noah called in the animals,
he was not the least bit frantic,
holy mariner that he was,
anticipating the ride. It was then
that I could imagine zebras, giraffes, and deer,
straining to hear, anxious. Sometimes,
if it were raining and we could not go outdoors,
my aunt would bring out her grandmother's quilts.
This one took two years, she'd say,
unfolding the silk log-cabin, its colors yet alive,
delicious as pineapple or lime sherbet.
But this one took a lifetime. We knew.
We'd seen it before. We'd looked at
the graveyard quilt, its twelve coffins
brown in the border like moored wooden boats,
and knowing the story, we would watch
a woman by firelight moving two small boats
up the Ohio River to the graveyard
in the center of the quilt, then embroidering her sons'

names in brown. My aunt loved the quilt. She'd hold
it to her face, and breathe. Much later,
my father told me about a dream
he'd had when I was a child. How he and my mother
take out a small boat, forgetting their child
asleep on the bed in a square of light,
they are fishing, needing to talk, it is afternoon,
the child's brown arms are outspread like wings,
then in the doorway, fragile as glass,
the house is a boat ajar.

BROKEN SYMMETRY

In the Museum of History and Science,
our guide challenges us:

quilts from this period
always have intentional mistakes,

but finding them is like looking
for needles in haystacks.

We accept the challenge, smile,
drop anchor, our eyes scanning each

feather, vine, and fossil
of the intricate cloths like radar

searching for storms, for ancient ships
lost at sea. We think

it doesn't really matter,
but find we're beginning to anticipate

algae, a green slip turned this way
instead of that, sails, stem up,

rather than down, visible signs of land,
a floating branch, a bird. We navigate

the walls of the museum,
our faces turned into the fabric,

two-hundred years old, still asking.
Later, at home, I think of Japanese potters

marring elegant vessels, still damp,
with their thumbs,

a row of hickory trees in Louisville
and the tornado that laid them flat,

white bones of fish fragile as hair,

my neighbor's second daughter Anne
wishing for the hand she was born without.

SHIP'S WHEEL, PRAIRIE STAR

1

These recurring dreams:
at the laundromat, two yellow
washing machines rocking in unison.
A woman quilting recklessly,
a ragged star pointing in all directions:
Buffalo, St. Louis, Los Angeles, Detroit.
Her husband in a yellow Volkswagen,
head bowed, quiet for once,
on the Watterson Expressway
or at the breakfast table. He's heard.

2

The space-shuttle Challenger explodes
like a bomb. January 28, 1986.
We watch it thoroughly on TV.

3

Sometimes I am convinced
there are no stars over Louisville.
Our houses cannot protect us. A country
the size of Massachusetts threatens us
with war. A schoolteacher
with brown hair, children,
a kind of naive ambition,
is dead. As always the dream
is skyward, landweary, expansive.

4

That day a woman's husband is late
coming home from work. She pretends
she is a compass, starfish,
a colored map of the city, turns down
the radio, loves him, stands at the window
watching the darkening street.

SUNSHINE AND SHADOW

for Dick Scobee

In bed, my son and I (he has talked
me into lying down with him
because it may storm) says, you can hear
it coming, and I can too, remembering
when thunder was like a distant plane
or the sound of the word "possession."
Then I had never seen an olive tree,
nor walls stained with light, though I had placed
red poppies on the dresser in a white bowl many times
to sleep and toss and listen to. Then

he'd come,
the soft slam of the car door,
his safe entry into the house, his coming,
in particular coming back to me, and my son,
his child,

asking now (since he is safe with his head
on my arm) what is the color of heaven,
but before I can answer, he answers himself,
both light and dark, and I wonder (when
he is surely asleep) could the man
have survived his fall into the sea,
is he well, unbruised,
might morning find him in the stem of her arms
riding his delicate, fast machines godward,
as if they were I?

THAT PART OF WOMAN

IT IS WHAT MAKES A WOMAN
NOT WANT TO SAVE HER OWN LIFE

for Margaret Fuller

That part of woman
that is hair and curtains is a part of wind
and remembering what makes things move,
and moving the wheat and cornsilk,
the foundations of houses.

(And when the ship settles
at the bottom of the ocean,
her strands of hair and fingers and seaweed
floating up water, floating)

And where is it that is happy?
Women's voices at the river and spinning
and lifting their dresses, and storms, the terror of storms,
and splashing to the thighs in the river.

(The color of burnt marigolds, walls
and standing in a room that burns down
around her, and placing gold bracelets
on her arms and dancing, dancing. The walls burn down
around her)

And when they move the old houses,
the houses rock back and forth
as if on waves, hot, black water,
small ships
moving out of town
late at night down Locust and out Main Street
and watching, the women, the procession.

EMILY DICKINSON HAD A LOVER
AND SHE NAMED HIM MASTER

There was something definite
about her hands,
and her face, angular, like mine.
(Emily, the way you loved that man!)
No need for maps,
but blueprints were another matter.

The beams of the house,
each joist, each cross-board, the empty spaces in-between
all fit like the sanctuary of my hands, or hers,
poised for his face.
(He was there, wasn't he?
And you took him to the attic, didn't you?

Talk to me.)
Angels strike out like birds. They hit the roof
and crumple. (Ssh, somebody will hear, you say,
and lead him down the stairway.)

Emily Dickinson knew this house,
the creaks and turns, thin stains on the walls,
bulbs deep, safe in the garden, and how blank spaces
on the page suggest doors and rooms, invisible
as air until they're built.

Even so, she would invite him in:
an ordinary man with skin more wine than white,
and hair the color of old wood. She would bring him to
  her house,
which, harnessed into rooms she' d spent her life in,
would spring to a skyscraper deliberately blasting the air
or slam to the ground, a confusion of shingles and wings.

EMILY DICKINSON TALKS TO T. W. HIGGINSON

What if I had come to you in white,
barefoot, intentionally
alive, your formidable objections
my private joke; my sparrow,
your prize. And when you told me
a dead boy means just that,
a fallen tree, I would not have flinched,
but loved you still, face to face,
sincere as any word, or bride. Or
instead of arranging irises in a vase, I had
chosen an exotic bird, more sapphire
than blue, or hearth, then worn him
as my winter coat, my plume. What if,
instead of summer yellow,
instead of good heart,
instead of anxious eyes,
I had come to you, practiced, in person,
sharp as a dahlia, or some terrible law,
counting on your awe?

IN A YELLOW ROOM ON THE SECOND FLOOR

for Emily Dickinson

When she breathed, words in the attic
and on the pool in the garden like thin-legged insects

got in her blood, and she rode them to God
with the force of an Appaloosa, that rugged speed.

So young boys die,
and there is such small power really; it's war —

a friend's son lies down in a Virginia wood,
in March at night, he is awake, with rifle close

and sky moving through limbs of oak, huge and black
as loss. A woman writes her poems against the light,

these boys are her hands, coming undone. Each night
an orb of fireflies rises over her father's house

like the sun. The household, her father, sleeps.
The roofs off her words uproar.

NO ROOM FOR THAT

for Mary Cassatt

There was a time when there was time.
You reached for your mother's voice,
and in the cool cream of her dress, it was
a hammock between trees, a sky held up
in girlish arms. Someone shook a quilt, and how
like white waves it was, just before it
squared off on the ground.

People talked in other rooms.
An older sister, Katherine, wore ochre and pearl.
You remembered her for years at the washstand,
the womanly curve of her spine, the splash
of water as she rinsed, and how the green awnings
on the verandah weighed heavily with rain or snow,
how summer nights, your brothers casting
invisible lines for trout, and angry words
somehow connected in your mind.

You never sailed a boat alone on the Allegheny,
held a hot forehead to your lips,
kissed a man permanently, conceived a child,
halted with miscarriage, nor peeled back,
because your child was ill, the days of a year
like fruit. Your sisters did these things.

Once, when she was young, you caught Lydia
at the Opera, alive in a swirl of lime tulle.
You couldn't have anticipated becoming your mother's
mother, there was no room for grace, for charm;
even women who in our time peer
into the green faces of machines, grow old.
You couldn't have known. Nor could she. Nothing
prepares a mother for that. A daughter,
looking hard for a while at children,
then dutifully looking away.

AT FIRST, MARY CASSATT

I wanted to save the mothers and children,
all chintz and pineapple and hot, black coffee,
until I was older, until I could see them
past long weekend visits, my mother's reminding,
I am not my mother.
And because you knew women apart from their husbands,
apart from their children, I wanted to say
a girl picking apples, her arms caught in the daylight
or half-dressed at the washstand or arranging her hair
is irrepressible as a zeppelin.
I wanted to say,
yes, I remember, I was full of desire
and wanted a boy as if nothing else mattered.
But it was the mothers and children
I kept coming back to —
the child like a pear just after bathing,
the ill boy asleep, the rasp of his breathing,
and one girl's small hand at her mother's light talking,
a simple caress, to read, or to shush her.

IF YOU'D MARRIED EDGAR DEGAS

to Mary Cassatt

and had children,
things would have been different.

Striped bedsheets swing on the line
like dresses. A child hands you a wooden pin.
There is the color of the kitchen.
You'd have chosen sienna.
There is a blue bowl on the table
and a bottle of fresh milk.
There are cats, cantaloupes, cucumbers,
the remarkably young open as jars.

You are home at noon,
your son, your daughters in from school,
coats unbuttoned, artwork in hands.
They are thin as silverfish, or fern,
as the rice paper you sketch them on.
This day Edgar is off.
Dissatisfaction is a movement of mind.
"Andrew, Mary, Johanna, Ruth,"
you say their names to keep them.

A house with children bobs like a small boat,
a summer bouquet —
snapdragons, daisies, the yellow lily
dips and waves like the neck of a young giraffe.
The children, with their father, bring the flowers
to you, each March, on your birthday,
when you are tired, appreciative,
not painting.

POEM FOR THE EARTH, INSTEAD OF MY CHILD

*(I find that I have painted my life —
things happening in my life — without knowing.
Georgia O'Keeffe)*

I was practicing big sunflowers
and great stalks of corn
that looked like Illinois, or other
whole, lucky places I had been
when I was a child,
when I wanted one. You said
no. So I answered in
calla lilies, white jimson weed,
the flowers about closed women
opening, like shutters,
doors. Near forty,
I asked again, half understanding
by then, if you've lost your child,
as you had, the risk
is terrible. And then
I noticed bones. The sky
rushes through an empty pelvis
like seas. When you photographed
my hands, I held them coupled
and braided. I was talking to you
in hands; these are the furies
of self, of age, of human silence,
I said. You answered in kind.
I have painted bones.
Some with flowers,
most without. The skies,
hills, the roads from there to here
disappear in them
like hairline
fractures.

INNER SPEECH

*(When I found the beautiful white bones
on the desert I picked them up and took
them home too. Georgia O'Keeffe)*

The door to the English office opens
and closes. Two men walk in, talking.
Sarah, at the front desk, nods. I do not
know her well. She is perhaps an iris bulb
or a house sparrow or a luna moth.
We speak in passing at the mailboxes,
or when she, sitting,
turns from the computer to ask what I want,
to oblige. If I asked what she wants,
would she, like my mother,
dark as mahogany reply,
or like a sweater turned inside-out,
flat, blue and warm as light,
tell how, alone with time,
she talks to stones,
alert to what they have to say, to give,
to pull her in. Once I was in, home,
and the walls' low wails were heavy
as a husband abandoned and aching for sex.
Once I saw white pelvic bones in a photograph
and touched them, the blue ground
they lay on, thoroughly, somehow noisier
than gathered birds. Goldfinch
I am. It is thistle that I crave,
and the raucous crowd in the bleachers
at a football game, black African violets
on the windowsill, rosy winsome women
cheering me on.

FALLING AWAY, REMEMBERING HE'S THERE

(There are people who have made me see shapes —
and others I thought of a great deal, even people
I have loved, who make me see nothing. Georgia O'Keeffe)

I suppose he's sleeping now
in a small second-floor room with wallpaper,
a blue-yellow room with shadows,
the window shade maybe three-fourths down,
a streetlight blinks on,
and the room is dark, except what comes through the shade
from the streetlight at the end of the block,
maybe his wife is asleep beside him,
maybe she is clearing the kitchen table,
checking the back door,
carrying a basket of clean clothes up the stairs, before
showering, dressing, getting into bed. Maybe

she doesn't sleep with him anymore.
The dreams he still has. I am frail, ill. The air-
conditioner clicks on. I am in a room of apologies.
It is something from the Bible, a test,
my friend is dying
and I long to share my body with her. He wants
to understand this, so he touches my bones,
my skin, dry like eggshell, like chaff. Maybe I am healthy
as a hand. Maybe I spit the terrible green wreck
of my stomach into a shallow silver pan. We
have both seen that. We know what
it means. God help us.
We can't land.

WHETHER DAY IS MORE BEAUTIFUL THAN NIGHT

*(It was a beautiful early morning . . . the
blackbird flying, always there, always
going away. Georgia O'Keeffe)*

On the way there
the trees against the sky
are soft mustard on blue.
The day has a certain clarity.
I remember him dark like an overcoat,
the stone bridge we crossed to our house,
paths worn walking, an old mill,
his looking at me
as if I were good;

if I were in church
under the brim of my Sunday hat,
I could think of sunflowers,
wear presence of mind,
courage dense as living bone,

and forget what I wanted most then:
the pulse and nerve,
the ground aflame, as if I'd lit a match
and tossed it there.
To stay. Yes,
startled blackbirds crowded the sky

that spring day ten years ago
when I saw an acre of grass
change to white yellow jonquils in seconds,
and my husband, my love,
slipped out of his wool night like clothing,
curved around me,
as desired
as a man ever was.

HOW TO TEACH THE SACRED

(I kept the first alligator pear so long
that it turned a sort of light brown and was so
hard that I could shake it and hear the seed rattle.
I kept it for years — a dry thing, a wonderful shape.
Georgia O'Keeffe)

We did it differently.
His held hands and formed the outer rim
of a very large ring. His,
like a diamond anniversary band,
encircled a field, and the field was
cowslip, foxtail, hay, and the field,
like the spent vegetable garden
in our back yard, spawned snow. Then
his waited, checking tracks,
quail, rabbit, squirrel,
keeping, still as sentinels, as apple trees,
an early morning watch for deer.

Mine came into the room,
each with her own seed, pod, shell,
or alligator pear. I said
a roe is a small deer with antlers
the color of limestone, of bone,
that God lives in the red hills of New Mexico,
in New England,
in the black, wide dirt of Illinois,
that when I saw a man nearly twenty years ago
at the edge of an old fish pond
casting for something as significant
as our second child,
I loved him wildly as phlox.

His eventually cheered at the sight
of a buck half-a-field over,
sound as a dark, abstract bird.
Mine saw an elaborate stencil,
the rack of antlers like a winter tree,
and the world was completely silent,
cracked open for them all
like an egg of light.

THIS POEM

(To see takes time, like to have a friend
takes time. Georgia O'Keeffe)

This poem you cannot use
to carry eggs, or apples,
even green ones with spots
the late afternoon of a day
or morning, going somewhere,
anymore. It is the color
of a small chair in my living room
and the color of a flowerpot
and the color of the skin
of your ears sometimes
when we're sunning and the sun
is behind you, you're radiant.
I give it to you, my friend,
it is the bathing suit
you would rather not wear,
the telescope at the window poised
twenty-five years, the abacus
with its lacquered frame
and round, white beads,
and beds of gladioli,
plum, pink, mauve, and prune.
This winter day is cold,
but I can almost feel the sun,
our arms are brown, glistening,
and swimmers swim a little
to the left of us, like words,
a little off-center, unclear,
and something else:

this poem is for you,
for your kitchen table, perhaps,
or beside a chair,
or the heart of your dining room table.
Yes, there.

THIS IS NOT HOW LEAVING THE WORLD IS SUPPOSED TO BE

(There were many other things that I meant to paint.
Georgia O'Keeffe)

I wanted to bury myself in the great, soft underbelly
of God, or, at least, like Melville, glimpse
the white whale of a dress he wears.
Or fold in the middle of some significant act,
like flipping off the high-dive, or bearing a child,
or kissing a boy until my lips are tired of kissing,
or in catching the purple marlin, see the lions.
Or maybe go out old as the hills. Can my grandmother,
sedentary now, a glass of water by her bed, remember
Cherokee Park in the winter, long, white hills and trees,
and red-cheeked boys pulling sleds upwards? And then to fly again.
But surely not like this: I lie down (Gatsby's arms
are just now reaching into night) think maybe tomorrow I shall
apologize, forgive, turn over simply, sail light.

WHERE I LIVE

WHERE I LIVE

The kite in the elm
outside my bedroom window
is red, faded
like a female cardinal,
torn. The sky this morning
white with winter,

and I,
years away from Illinois,
from the red, brick house
my father built,
from my mother
and my sisters,
from the black, turned soil
of my grandfather's farm,

have locked myself
into the heart of a man.
From ladder
to roof
and to the nearest tree,
the higher I've climbed,
the more fragile
the branches.
From here,

I can see
the Louisville boys
unfurl their Confederate flag,
and the old railway bridge
like an iron thoroughbred
upon them,
the banks of the Ohio,
the slick red clay;
a girl is most lost
when she recognizes nothing.

I have wanted the earth flat,
the barge to slip northward,
the sky so close
I could touch its pale roses,
where the stems of the grasses
were the stems of my knowing.

Help me step lightly,
though I am neither lost,
nor going.

A FIELD OF TULIPS IN THE KITCHEN

I named you "Clint"
because in a slow dream a rooster pulled the red sun
                       out of the sky
with hands thin as rain,
and the edge of a cornfield fell not
                   off the earth
with a thud,
and your father one cold November morning
curled himself like a newspaper
                 into a brown antique quilt,
then six shiny tractors in green,
           then bears,
               then words,
then the slopes of hills,
slipped easy as soap through daytime
       that white-cracked door, or the moon.

SACRED SPACES

His favorite part of the house
is underground. There
one expects stalactites, bats, a guide
to turn out the lights,
then everything stops, dead. A crate
of old potatoes is on the floor,
the ferns from the eyes in the dark
grow down, then up, then onto
boxes of birdshot, lost onions, receipts.
His is where in this house once,
near daylight,
on an old railway bridge, trains
collided, derailed, where a boy,
years later, straddles the trestle, to see.
If I am pregnant with his second child,
pregnant as a winesap apple,
then full with child as a hot-air balloon,
our child is conceived because the first
is alive as periwinkle, and a bowl I love
falls off the dining room table,
ruined as a clay bird.
His is where we've stored the cradle,
the musical mobile: a melon slice,
a slice of pear, and six other blue singing slices,
and string, are there.

VEGETABLE SOUP

A woman gets that harried look.
She feels like fog. Blink, and she's gone.
Blink, she's back, tired as a bruise and rattled.

She makes mistakes, forgets things: her change
at the grocery, the red food-coloring she went for
in the first place. She can no longer think
of just the right word for the thing
at exactly the right moment. She knows "oatmeal,"
"spinach," "eggplant," "gorilla," and "umbrella,"
but no longer sees the connections
nor remembers her life of doing so.

She's heard she ought to take vitamins,
vacations, paint her toenails mauve.
Her mother says have another child.
That should fill you up like an A.

Like an A, she laughs remembering, the body for once
had a mind of its own. There was no such word
as "focus." Her head used to be a helicopter.

She'd been after the birdseye view:
the river, a ribbon. She could drink it,
ride it, admire it, wear it like the shiny red dress
it is at night when the cars are crossing over. All this,
and all the connections:
lines in a sonnet someone might draw,
a row of vegetable soup cans in the pantry,
a gentle red-haired man a distant city might sacrifice,
submit, trade, or divulge, to a woman at war, like a secret.

MY FATHER'S CHERRY TREES

I have painted my fingernails
for the first time in my life. I am
thirty-six-years-old, and my fingernails
are the color of moss-rose. You notice
and say I remind you of another woman,
a friend of ours. I emulate. I am trying
to please. How odd, after years of planning
just the opposite. In another room,
the children are in bed, the rowdy baths
over, like oysters curled in their shells,
silent, fragile fish, sleeping through
the night. Yesterday
my father took them through the woods
behind his house to a small farm
where there are cows: "horsies,"
my three-year-old was ecstatic.
We are city people, my children and I, but you
somehow know the difference between cypress, cedar;
cumulus, cirrus. Some things I have learned.
My father attempts cherry trees:
in Louisville in May he talks harvesting,
pie and cobbler, the land. You need
Wisconsin, I've almost told him, or Michigan,
where the sun is less cruel, and cherries grow easily,
waxy red and spotless. But he is undaunted,
and I indulge him. The cherries
will be wonderful this year, I tell him, fingering
the blooms, imagining rubies or garnets,
easier bruised, ethereal.

WHAT I THOUGHT WAS A BIRDHOUSE
IS REALLY A LAMP

for Sena

This poem begins as a birdhouse.
A white one with twelve holes, a porch,
and a roof. I wonder if there
are shingles on the roof and decide
yes because rain ought to roll
off a bird's house
the way it rolls off her back.
This particular birdhouse is designed
for martins. With the wings
of that purple bird we might estimate
our distance from the sun. I am
five feet two and a trillion wings
from the sun. A birdhouse generates
its own electricity. It is warm
enough to melt things. There is light
in the windows. "With the wings
of a redbird I could fly to God,"
my son at four is resolute,
serious as bread,
insistent that the birdhouse
be named his name.

LESSONS

Thursday afternoons in September
when it is cool and dark earlier each day
my son climbs the bleachers at the high school
while, on the football field, his father, quiet,
in his oldest clothes, paints white lines, markers
for the weekend's game. My son, yards away, lost
almost to sight, talks himself up the cold aluminum,
lights into stirrups of scaffolding
until to fall is unthinkable;
six-years-old is an air-borne plane.

I married a man one December when I was young;
his hair was the color of marigolds.
I knew there was truth in that, and
even though it snowed the day of the wedding, and
the roads were impossible, a field
of zinnias erupted in me
like a fireworks display. It could have been July,
another month and I'd be back at school.
Sometimes I am certain that I was.

In first grade, on his drawing papers, my son
wires houses for electricity, lights,
lights in every room. We know he is afraid of the dark.
As yet, no one has mentioned loss.
But when he draws his father,
he draws him intercepting a crucial pass,
hands on the sorrel ball,
jersey red like a firetruck. I see poppies, then,
apples, blood, the whole stadium is white with sun, and
every person in the bleachers, our son,
I, too, this bright fall day, learning.

THE PURPLE LADY POEMS

THE PURPLE LADY AND BIRTH

One time
the purple lady
curled herself tightly
into a tuna-fish can
because the world looked like
a large weeping woman
in a red blouse
and she could no longer
think of trees as her babies.

At that time
the purple lady found death easy:
growing small as a sperm cell,
black as night clutter
and all the caves curled up
inside the earth like dogs.
The purple lady entered
where beautiful women forget their faces,
the lights in the ceiling,
the men who touch
and touching back the men.

Who is to say
what made the difference —
jelly of skin, bone, teeth, smell, God,
the baker sifting his white dust
over the floor of the cave?
The purple lady unwound her body
and ate the wide air
until she was as tall as her mother
leaning toward rain,
slash, fire
sparkle, breath.

THE PURPLE LADY AND SEXUALITY

1

Her mother and father bore six sons
before the purple lady
was conceived
and being near fifty
the two delighted in their girl child
and offered her sweet womanhood for breakfast
like slices of melon.

2

The purple lady loved her brothers,
she loved to watch them
wash the sweat off their bodies at noon
before coming in the house
from baling hay or planting corn.
Water and light
made the bulk of their backs,
their chest muscles shine.

3

Because it was time
the purple lady envied her brothers
and ignored the black glassy urn
glowing inside her body.
And because she desired it
no breasts grew
and there was no rounding out
nor making of comfortable houses
for young men to come in,
sell their goods,
leave happy.

4

The purple lady at seventeen
became her daddy's green flashy tractor
that digs the farm,
readies it for planting.
The purple lady
with bags of tree-sprouts in her pockets
and gold feathers pinned to her skirts
is pushing west her ancestors' fields.

THE PURPLE LADY AND THE GARDEN

This is the last image she has of her grandfather.
He is at home on the front porch,
the metal glider is red and where the paint is chipped,
it's aqua. He is holding a silver tumbler
of icewater, half-wet on the outside,
and she wonders if his hand is cold,
holding the cup so still.

Her father has told her there was always a garden.
Behind the house, a quarter acre from the barn,
a quarter acre itself,
there was lettuce in the early spring, then snap beans,
squash, turnips, corn, and finally sweet potatoes,
row after row, to last the year.

She can imagine her grandmother and him harvesting
his last crop, she in a blue cotton blouse, nearly eighty,
resting upright in the sun, her grandfather pushing
his old shovel, again and again, into the soft dirt,
then brushing off the large orange potatoes, three, maybe
four inches in diameter, predictable,
firm, and sweet.

Once her father said he could never work a day in the sun
without thinking of his father. Later he said
that the smooth wooden handle of his father's shovel
had chilled the inside of his hand
when he'd picked it up, and he'd thought
of that old house, quiet as winter, and his father
sitting with him when he could not sleep,
talking to him, telling him stories.

THE PURPLE LADY AND GOD

1

Panic circles the rock
lights on water
nervous as a wasp, is quiet

and God is a woman, her eyes
the color of linen. And God loves trumpets
and words and sand dollars to wear
around her neck, and sand
to step upon.

2

When God is a man
he straddles the top of a mountain, and talks,
his voice filling your sorrow
with red, red language,
a noise so grand
you believe the mouth of God
is at your ear,
and inside your body
making it move.

3

The purple lady keeps a shell and a wing
in a glass box on her table.
At night
a black butterfly
emerges from the box
and makes a journey
from her red-walled rooms
and from all the waiting gathered in bundles
by the door.

One must take off her fear like clothing.
One must travel at night.
This is the seeking after God.

THE PURPLE LADY AND MARRIAGE

Sometimes
the purple lady knows
she is her mother's daughter.
She sees it in her own brown eyes
and in the wandering blue vein
just below her left clavicle.

She remembers her mother
in a gray or black or brown dress,
her father's insisting his wife wear no color,
and imagines one day, out shopping,
or somewhere else, running into her mother
in a coat so red
it hurts to look at it.

When she married,
the purple lady wore a simple dress,
her grandmother's locket, new shoes.
She wonders if her mother, upon saying her vows,
listened as she did, for running faucets,
a snow of moths,
and over her head and the chapel,
even over love,
the low insistent argument of planes.

The dress hangs in the closet
in a white, plastic bag. Sometimes
she takes it out and touches it. For him,
her beauty had nothing to do with dresses
who still touches and moves her "sweet jesus"
as imaginatively as a boy.

Still,
she hears her mother's warning about insects.
She is considering having the dress cleaned
or washing it with mildest soap
in the kitchen sink,
like an infant.

THE PURPLE LADY AND PREGNANCY

From her window she can see the lake,
sunlight in morning, and shadows later,
and these things of childhood:
black soil, wheat bending in the distance,
her mother's father Daniel who died in his sleep,
a piano, a river, fish iris and silver,
and sun moving toward night into months,
maybe years.

The unborn child is a cellist on a chair
inside a pool of water, instrument and arms poised,
head tilted. You have known her shuffling about
early mornings on cold kitchen floors,
and in brief memories:
a mother at the clothesline, a father's dark smile,
his darker words behind.

Sometimes, before sunup, the purple lady
is awakened by strange, sad music, and a certain fear,
but then she imagines her daughter's breathing water
easily as air.

THE PURPLE LADY AND MARY

Sometimes the face of Mary
is in the folds of the purple lady's clothing.
Mary is looking out, her eyes
the color of pheasants, somewhat bewildered,
or she is answering all of our questions
in whispers.
            Goya of free hair,
dark tressed Jew, there is no thought,
only wet black leaves
and windows, the tree breaking at center
during a storm, our children leaving.

THE PURPLE LADY AND POETRY

Each time
it was like stepping
into her mother's old party dress,
the seafoam green with dots,
and the attic walls were low
with just enough light,
and her mother was downstairs,
circumspect as a pearl, calling up,
"girls, are you all right?" and
Kathy was there too
in the fuschia and gold, saying
"zip me up," and she was
alive as a grasshopper,
uncharted as the moon then.

And it was like stepping
into the Pacific Ocean
with its heady pull
and making believe seaweed
is lost mermaid's hair,
and she could remember
sitting, before bed,
on the living-room floor,
her mother brushing 98, 99, 100 times
her hair, and her mother
was well again
with lungs full as taffeta.
It was like that too.

And it was like sex,
the first time in a rented room,
all risk and applause and god,
and after that
it was calligraphy, or air,
and after that
the egg and sperm calling one another
like whales.

It was what she wrote about —
life full as a mouth whispering,
"it's good, it's good; stay,"
and death administering,
just as a father.

Maureen Morehead's poems have appeared in journals, including the *American Poetry Review, California Quarterly, The Iowa Review, Poet and Critic,* and the *Southern Poetry Review.* Her poems have also been selected for inclusion in the anthology, *Selected Kentucky Literature,* and she has received numerous grants and honors for her work.

She received M.A. and Ph.D. degrees from the University of Louisville, and is currently teaching in the Jefferson County, Kentucky, public school system. She lives in Louisville, Kentucky, with her husband and eight-year-old son.